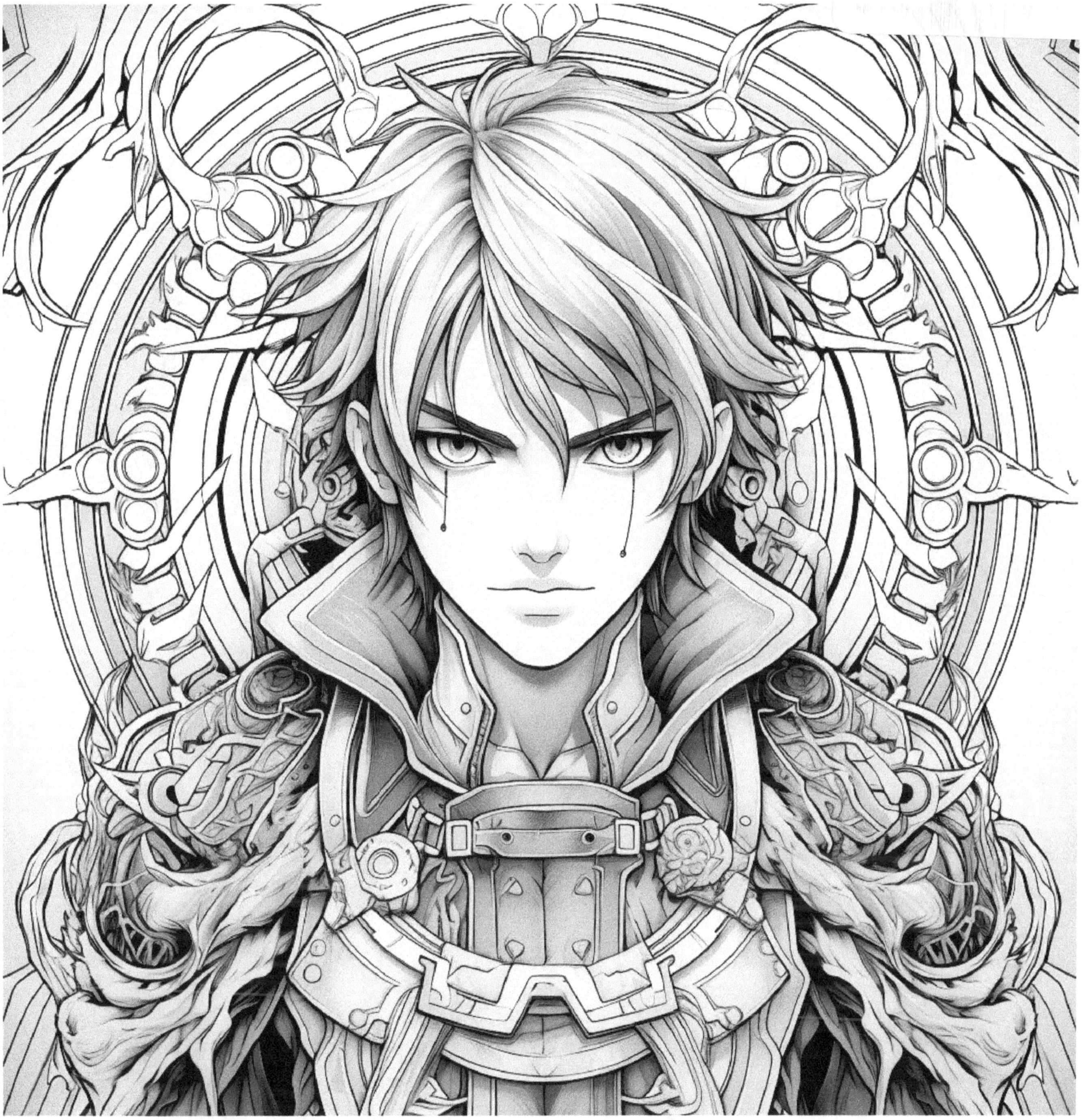

THIS COLORING BOOK
BELONGS TO:

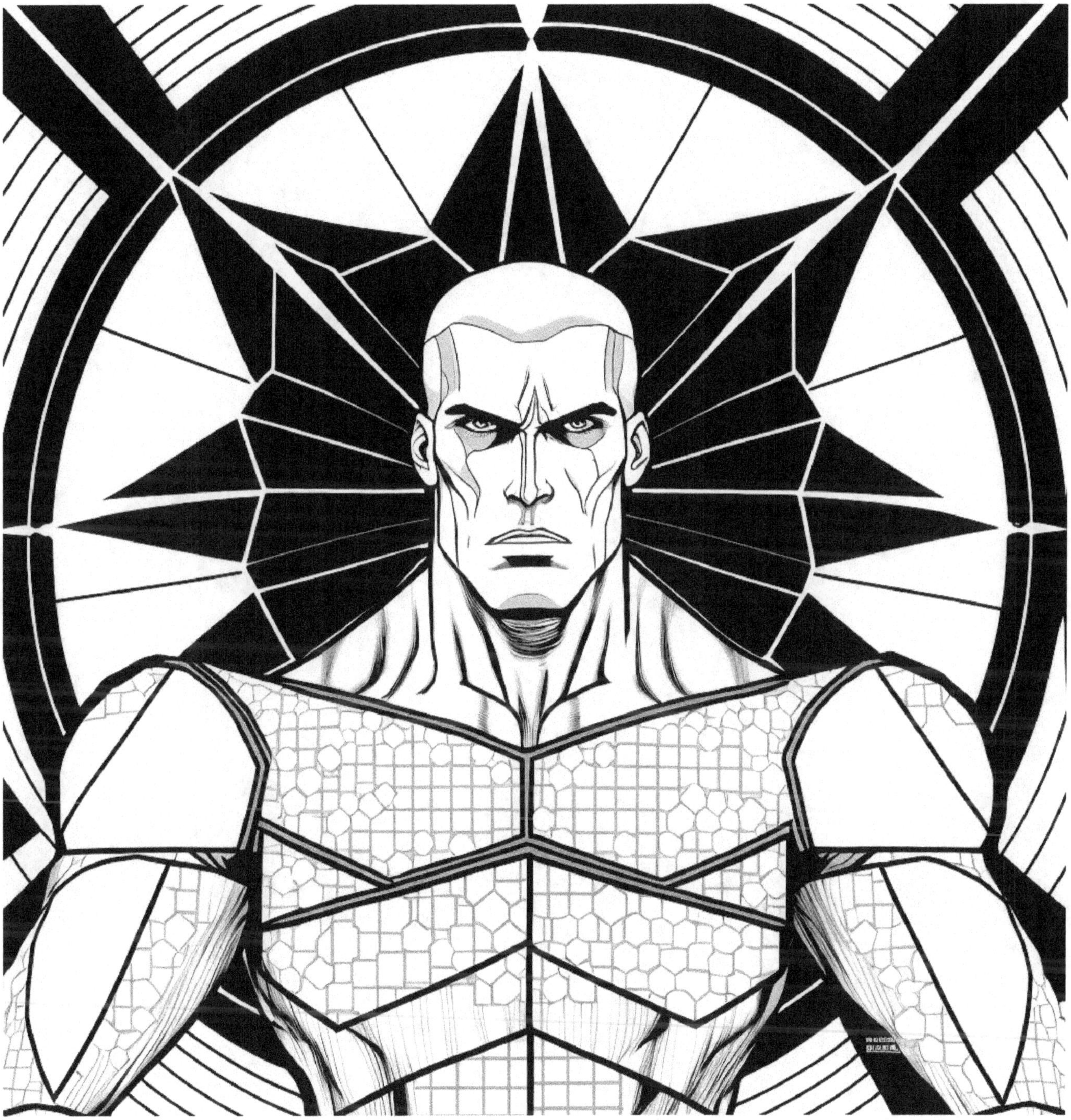

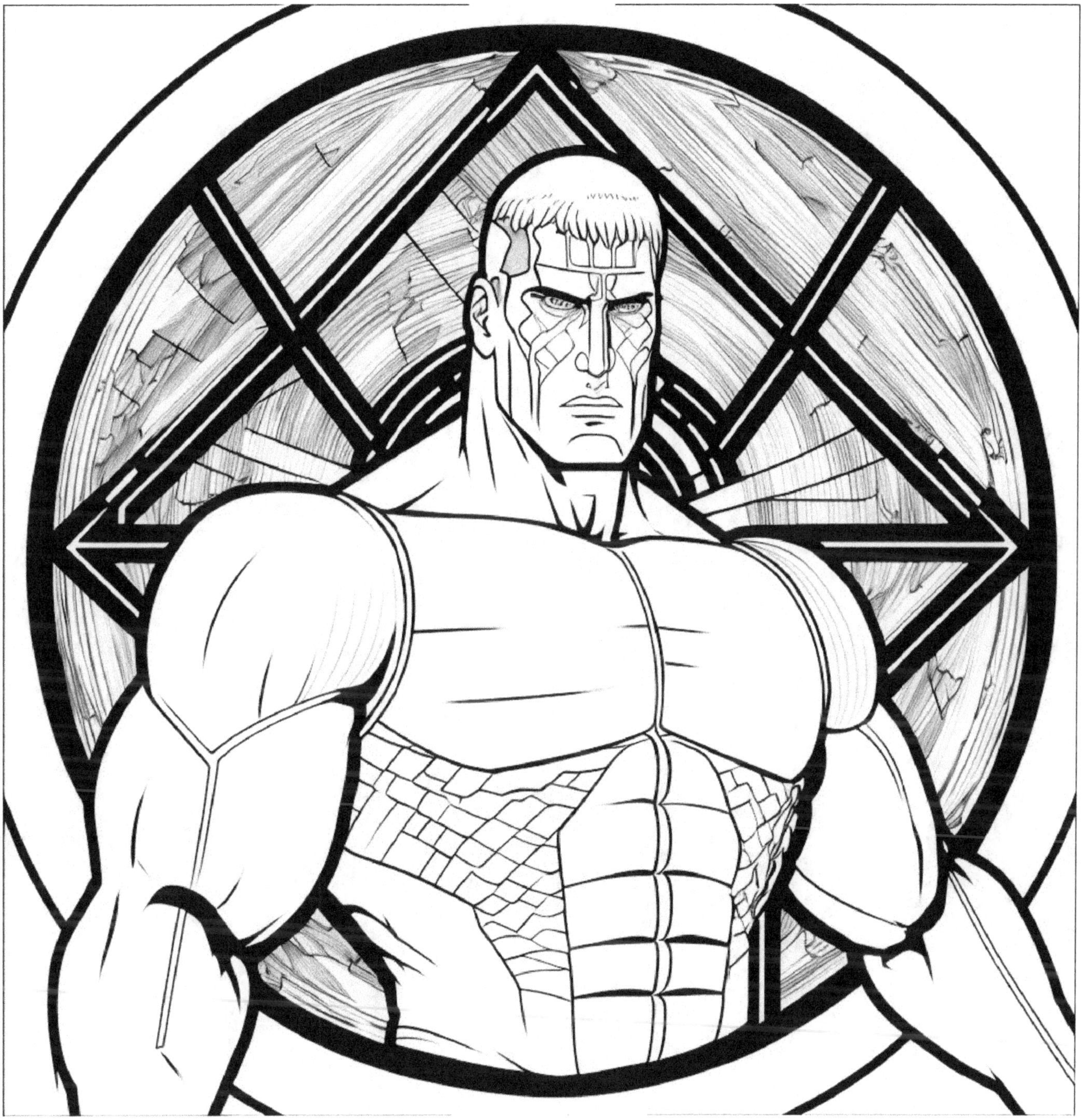

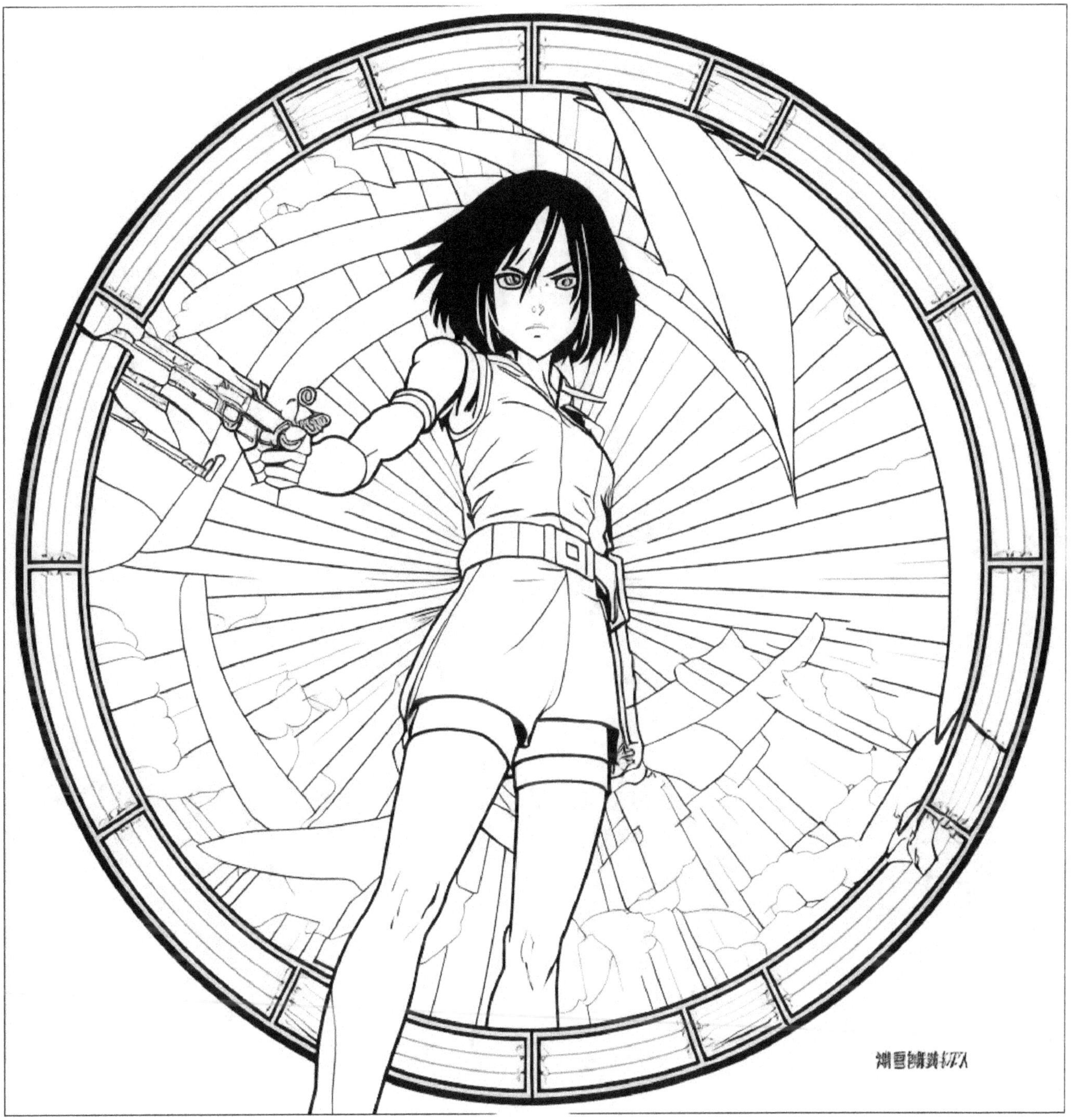

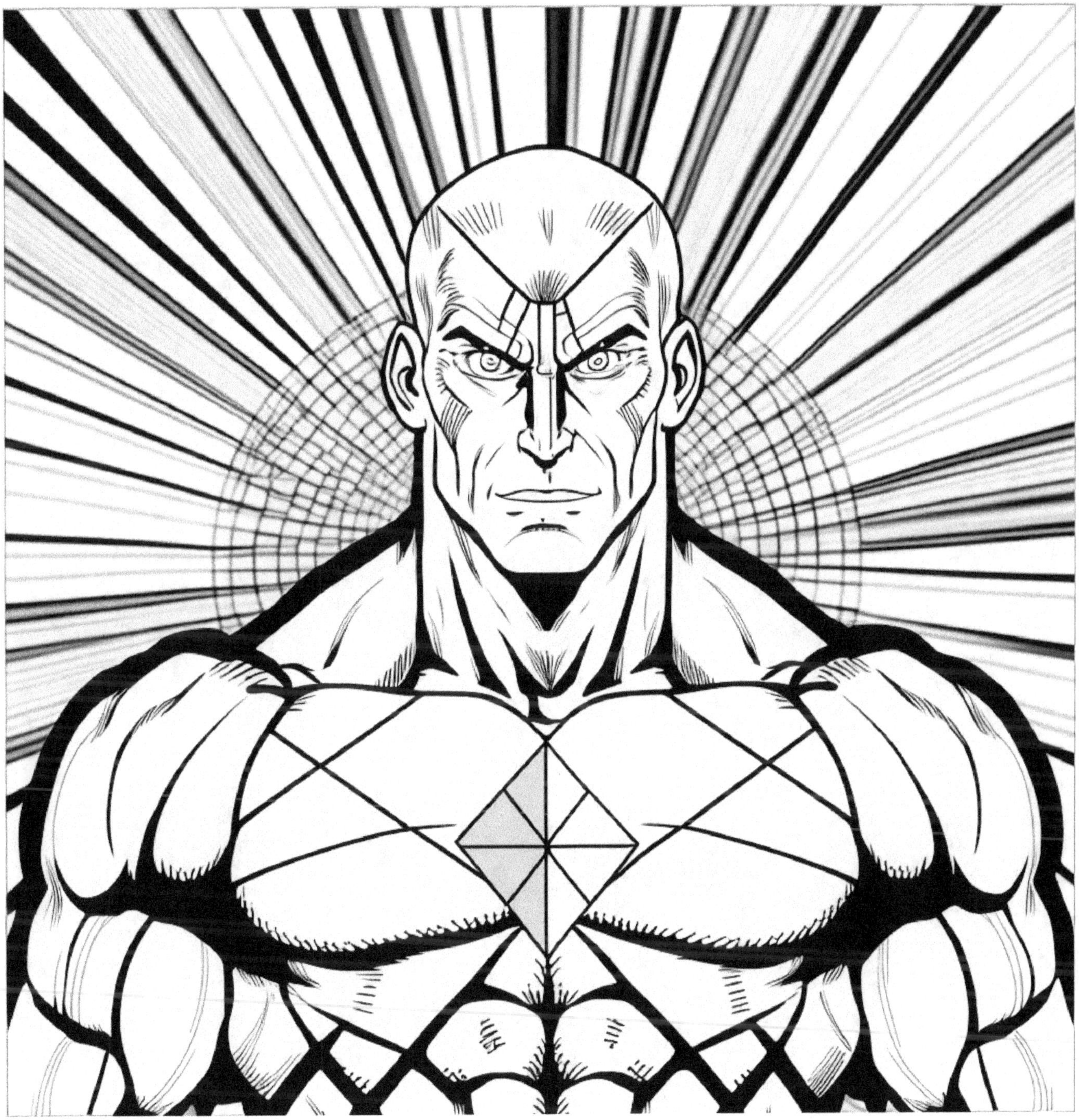

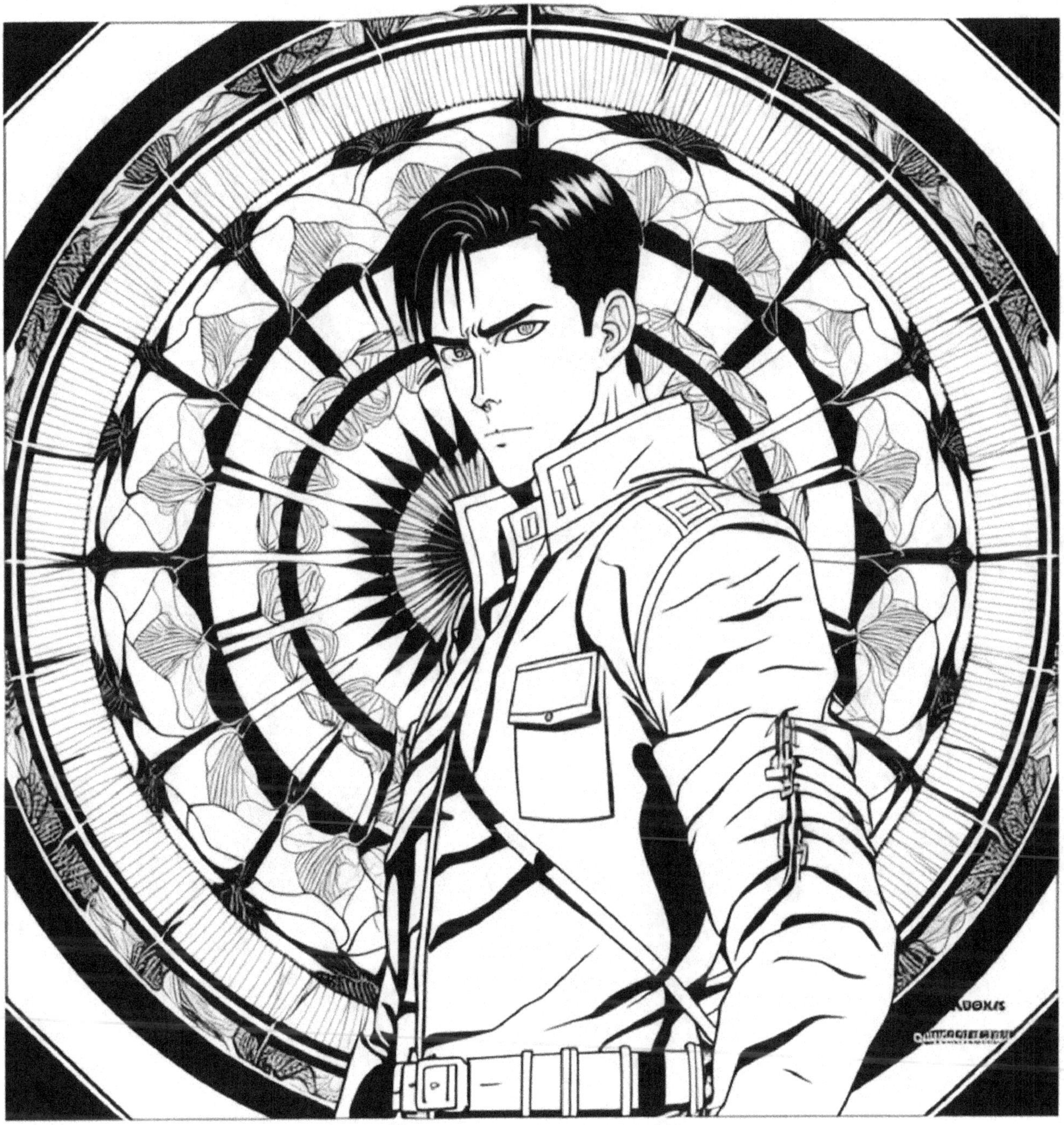

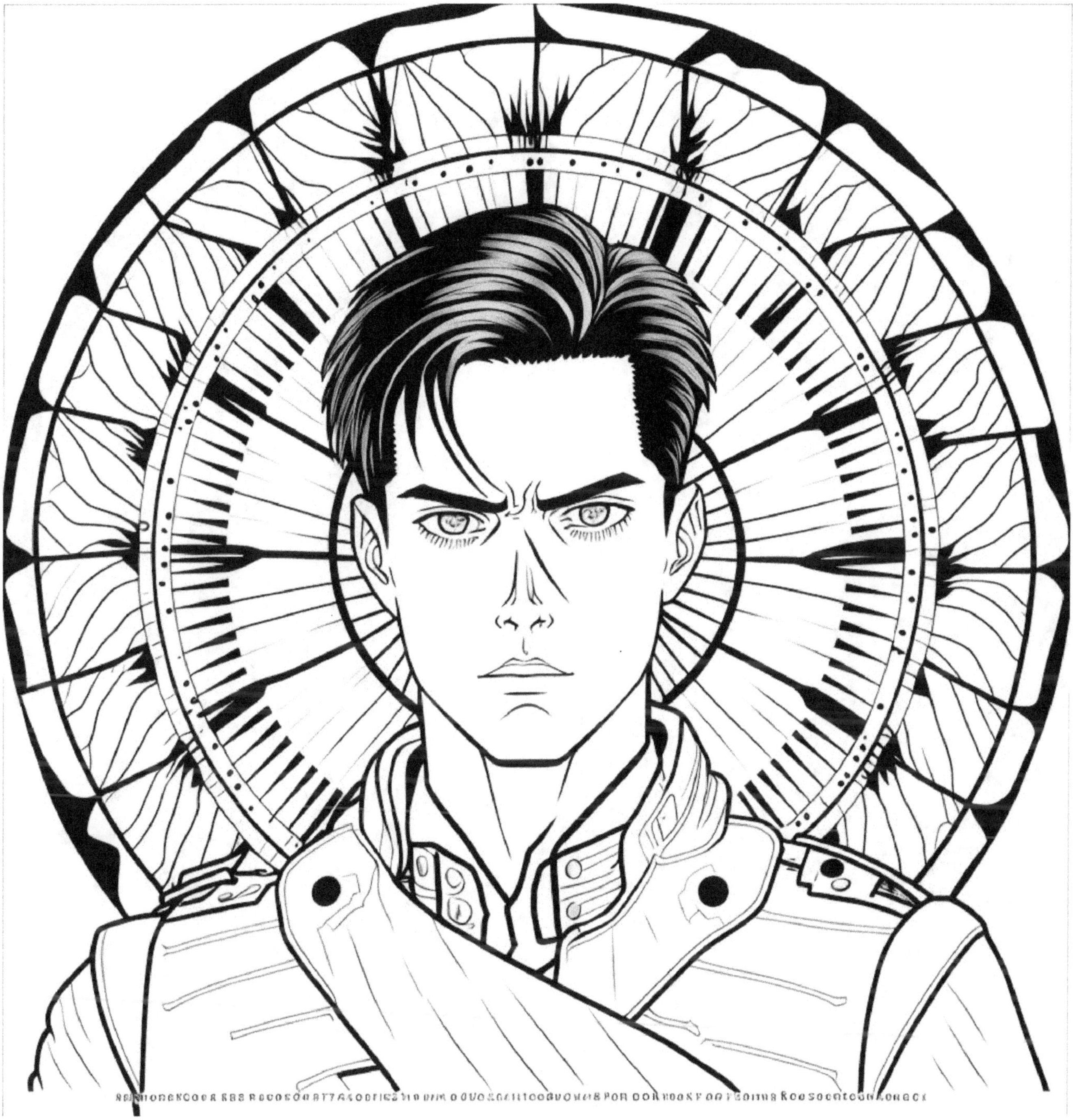

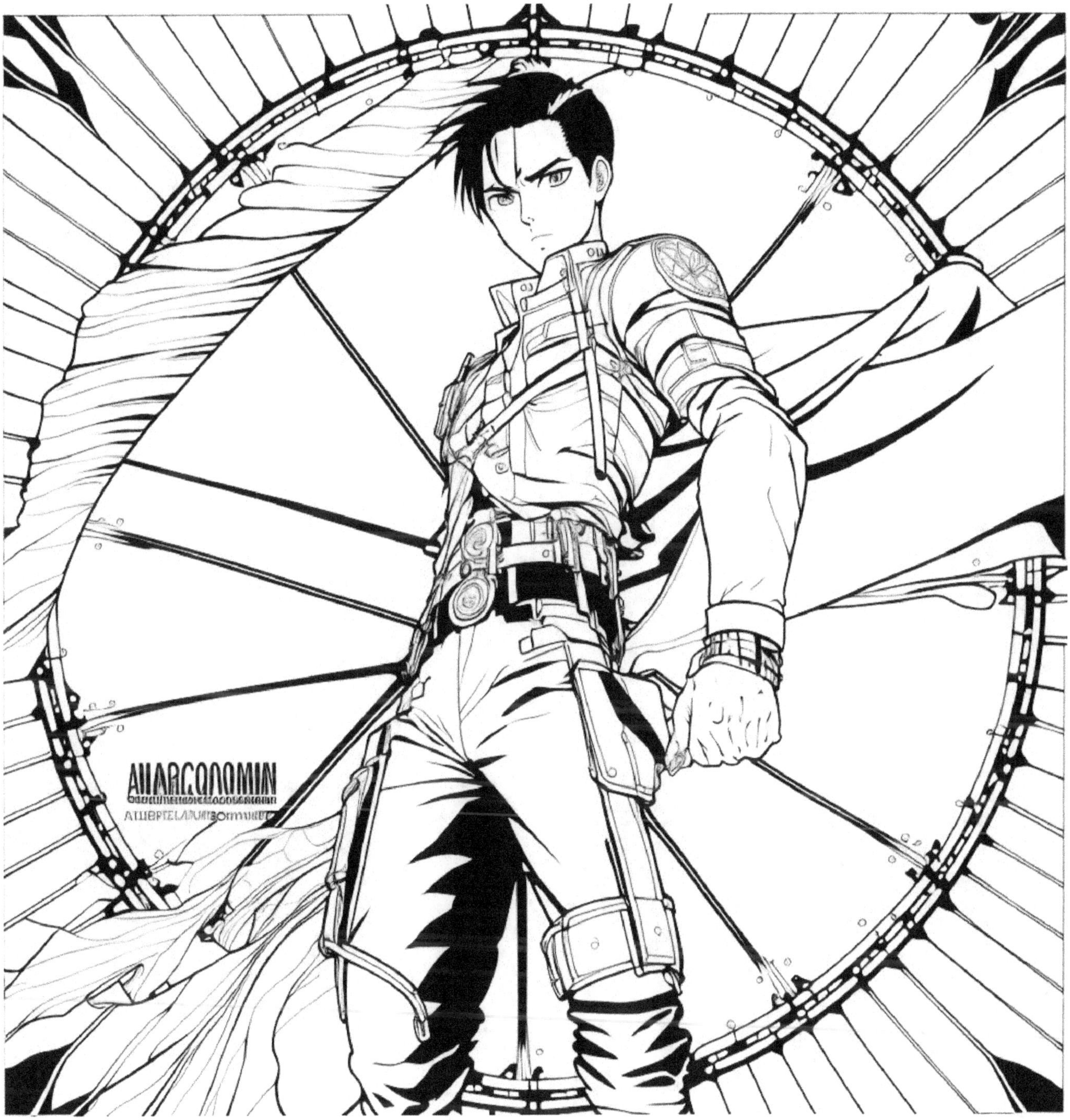

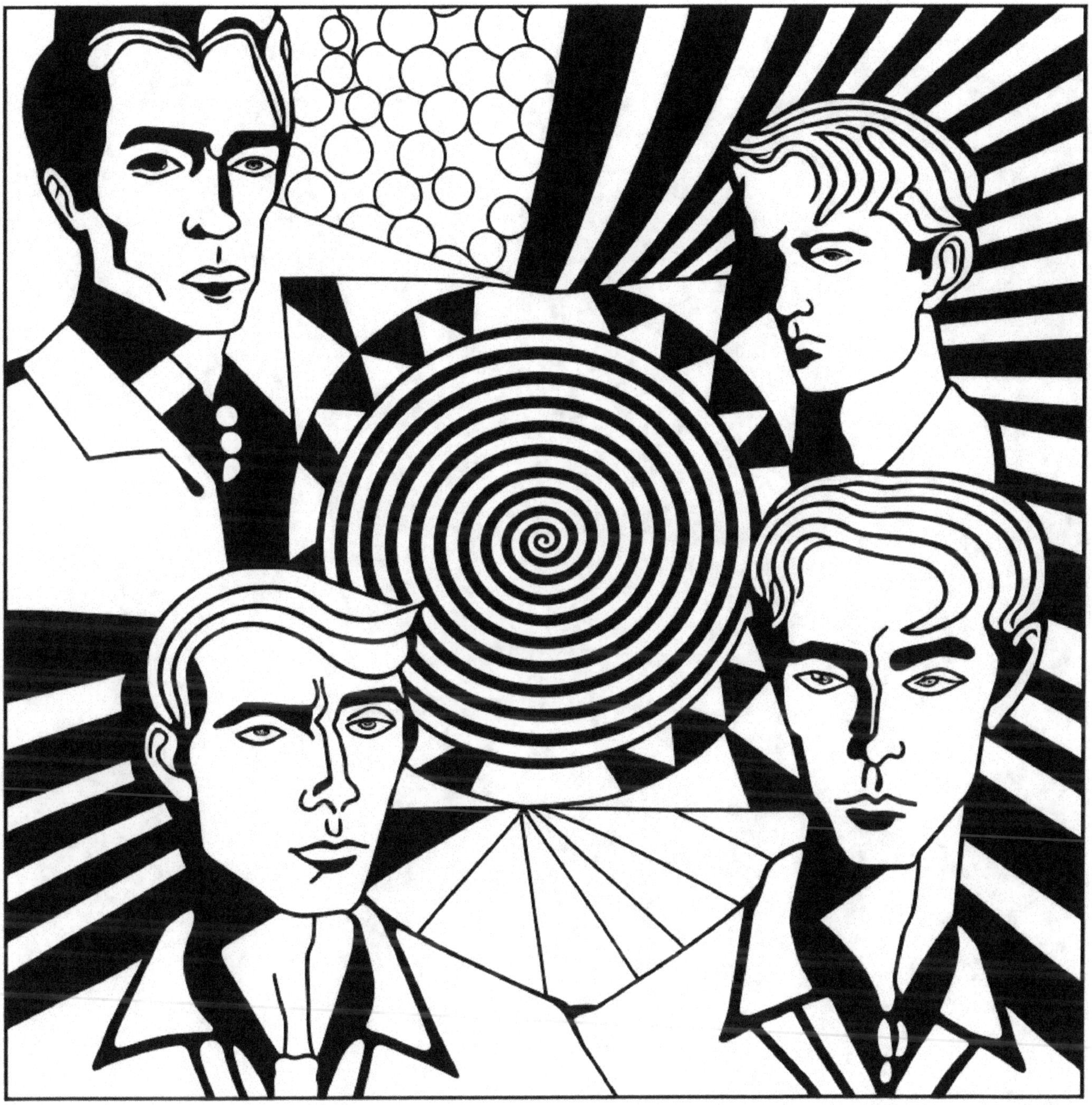

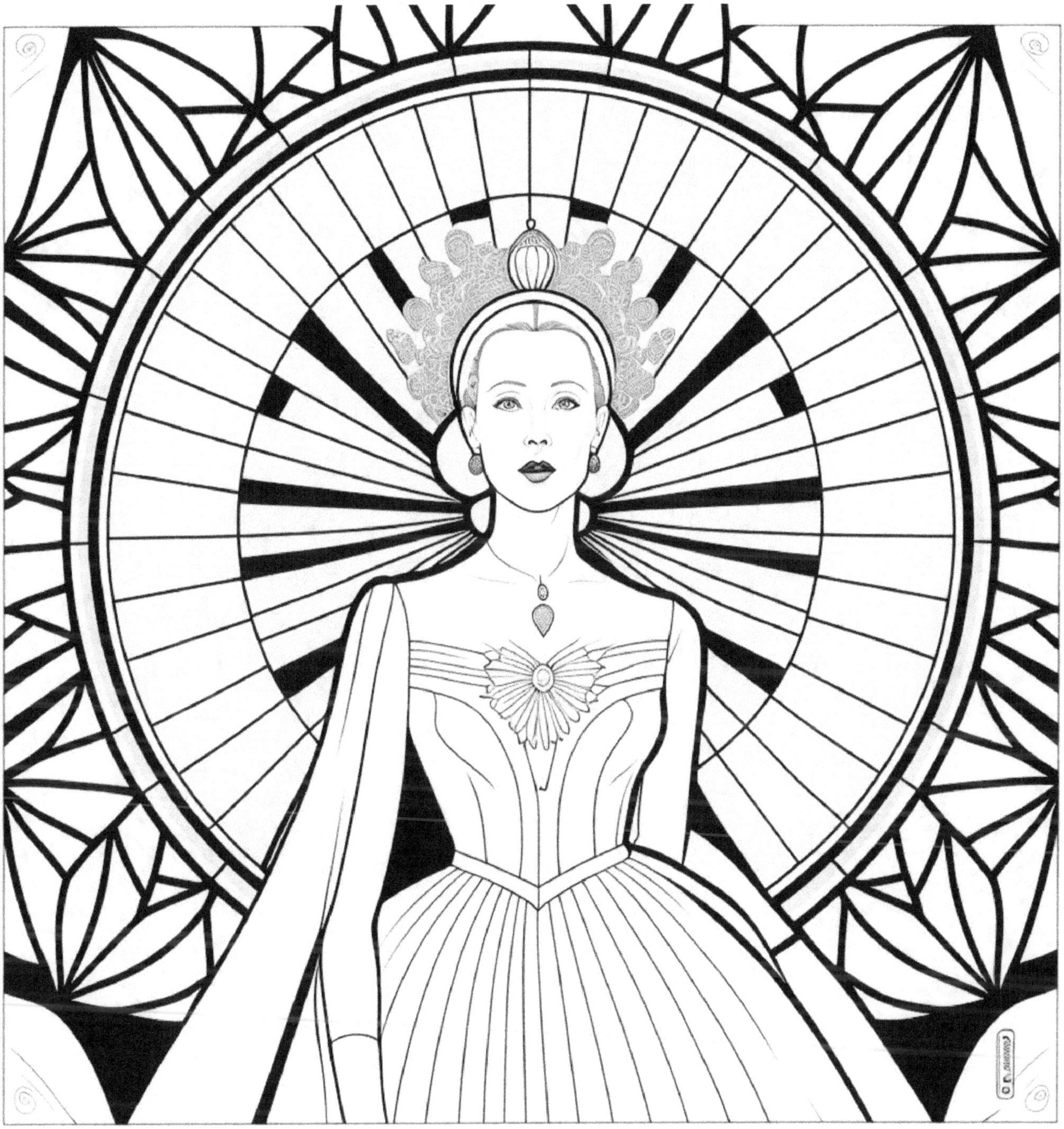

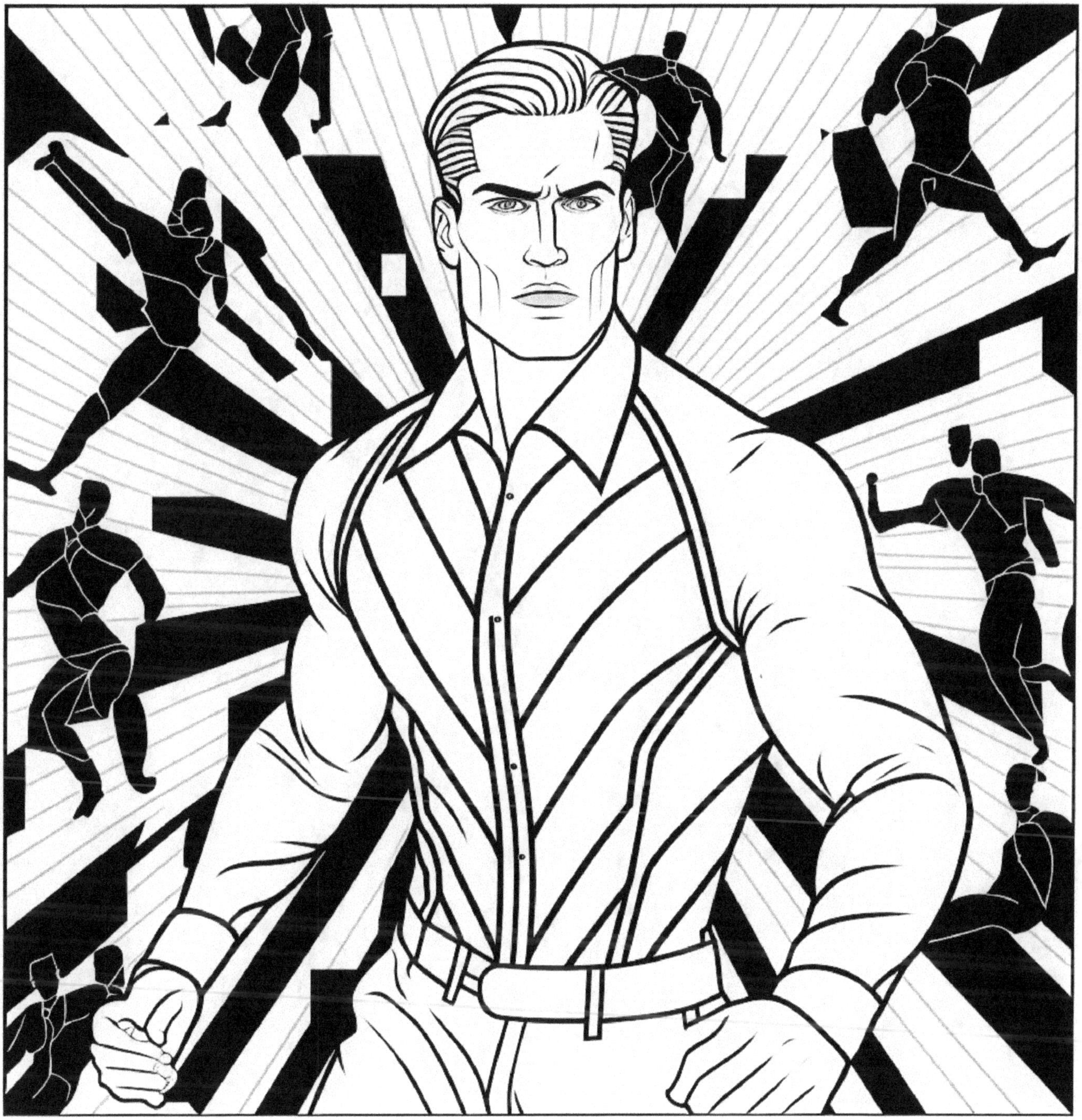

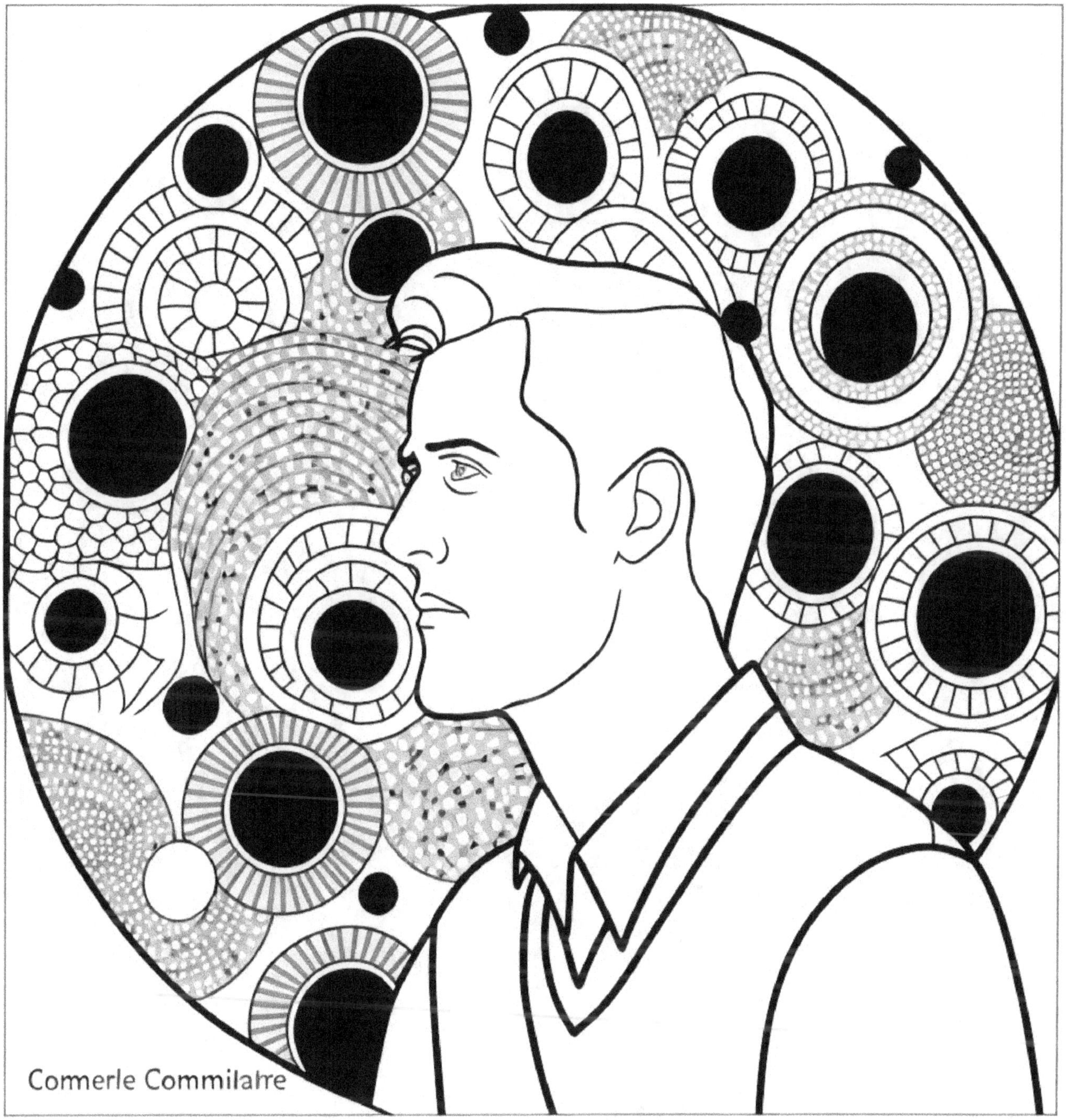
Comerle Commilaire

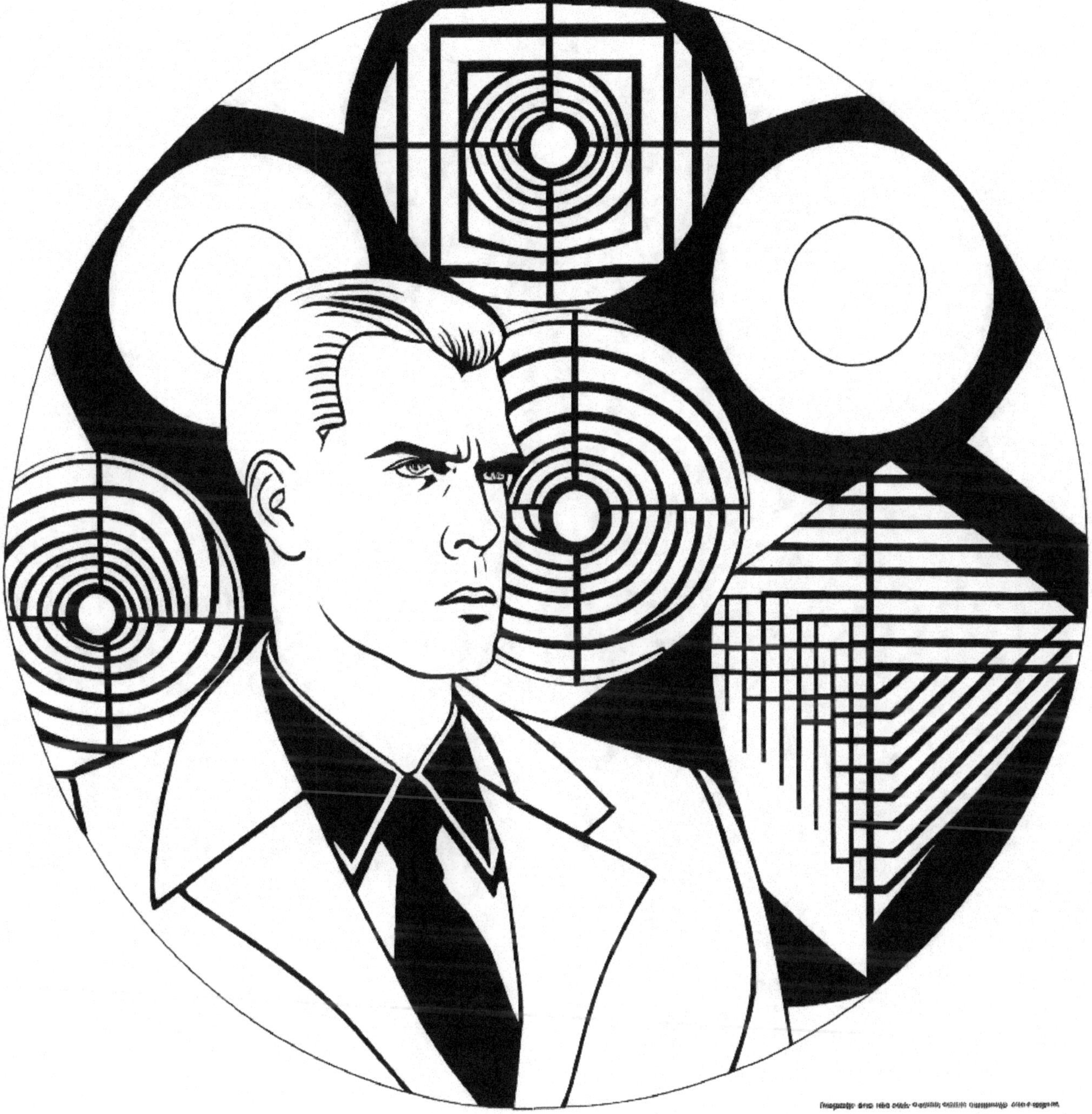

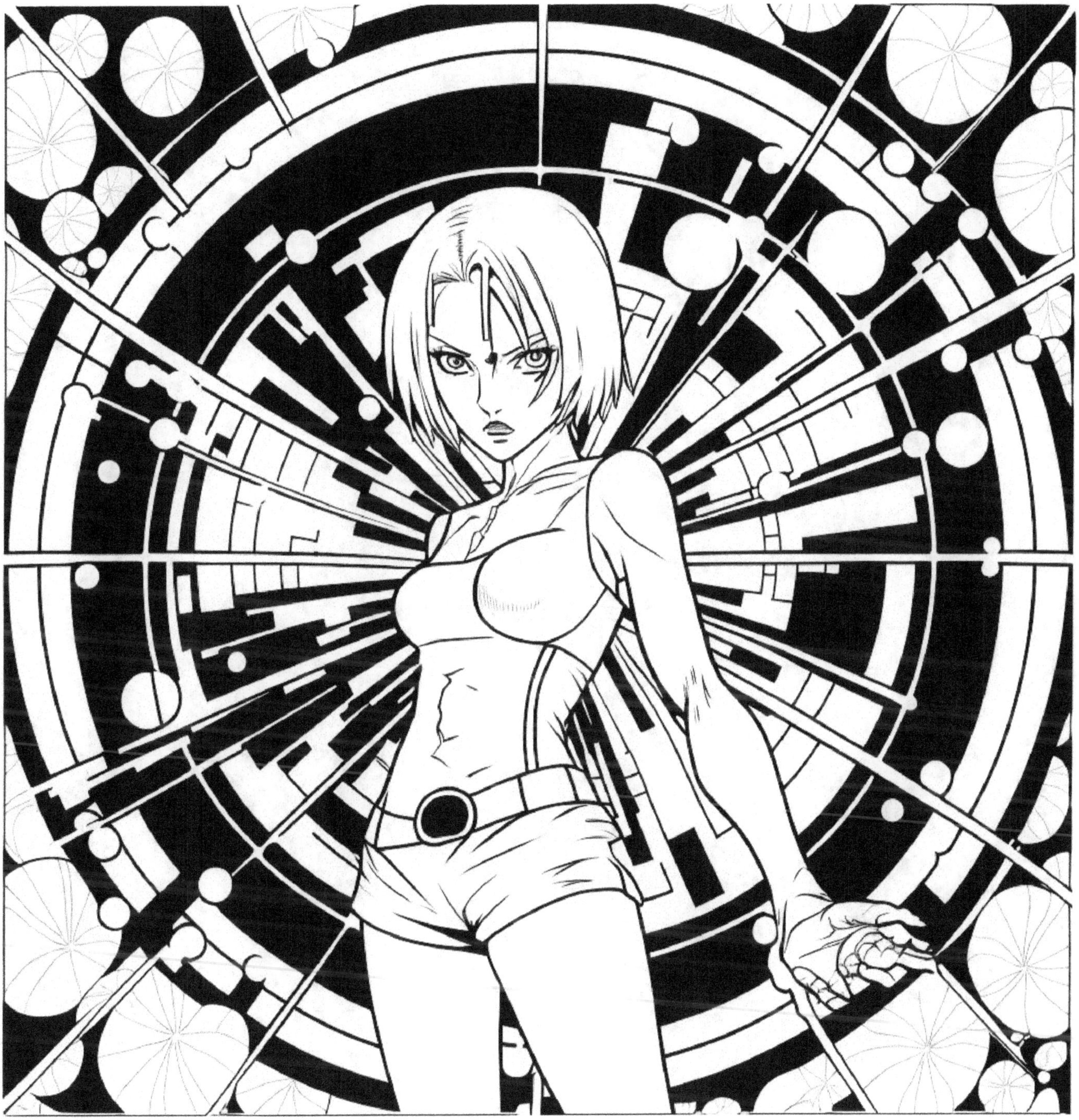

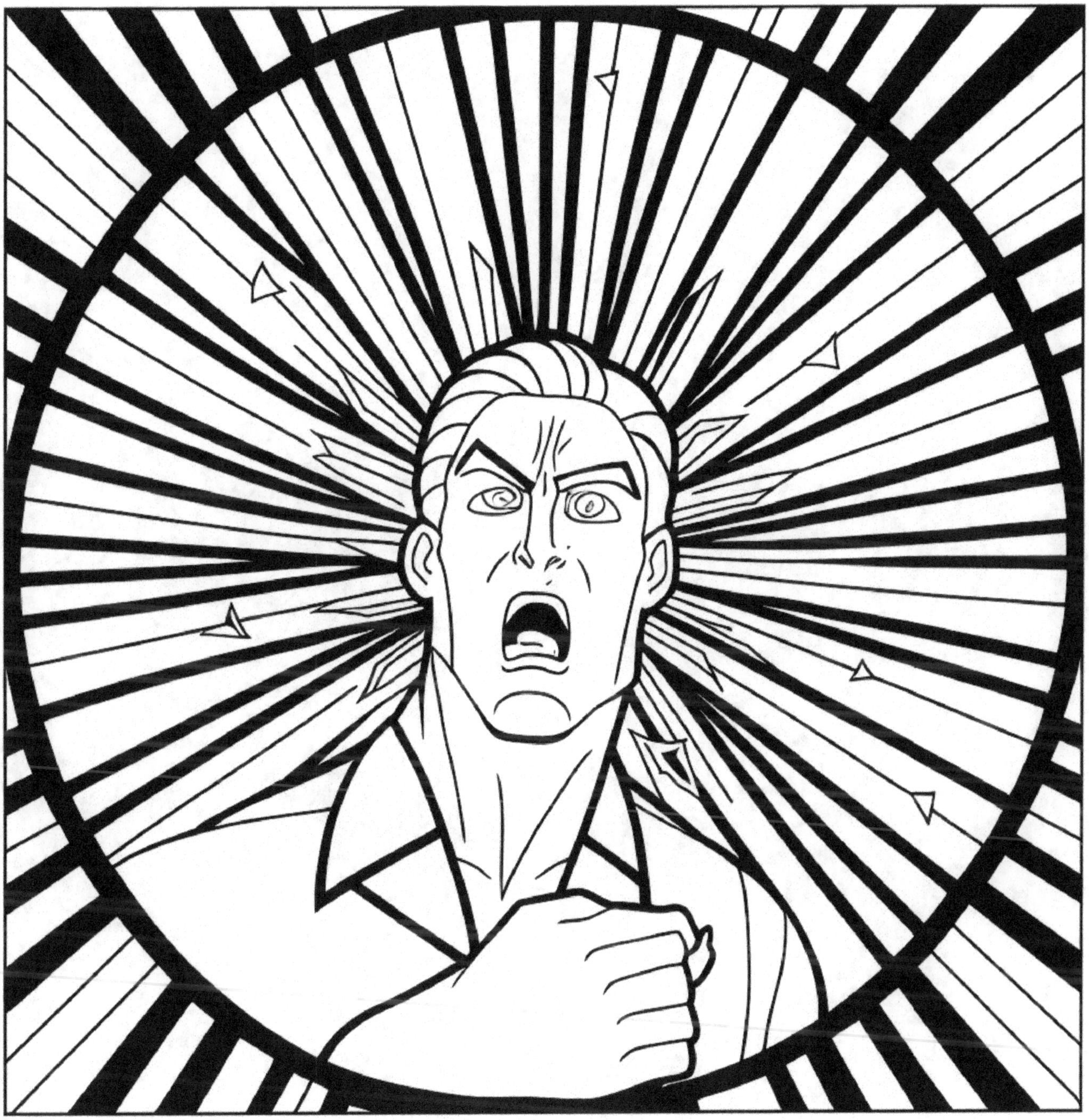

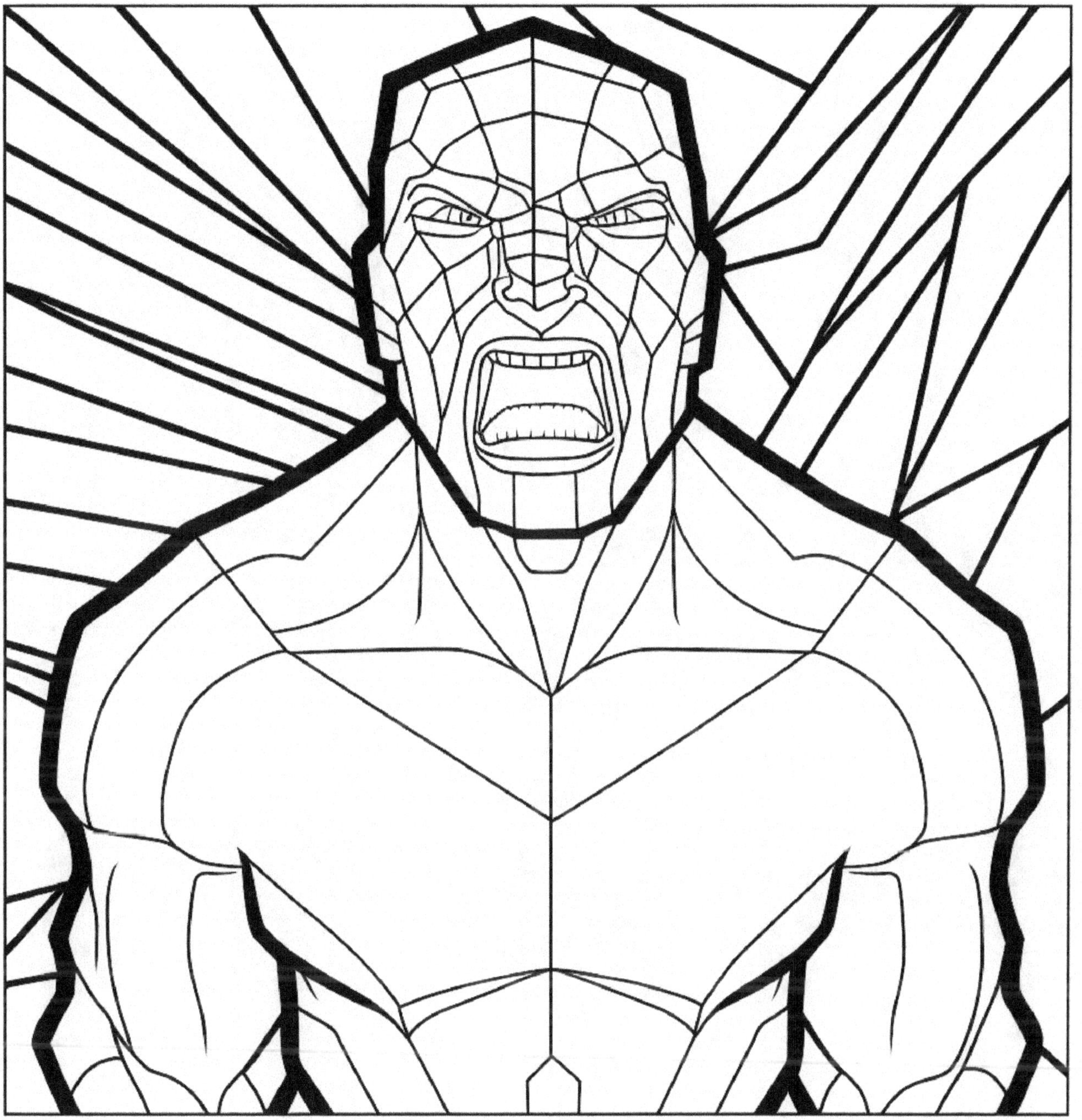

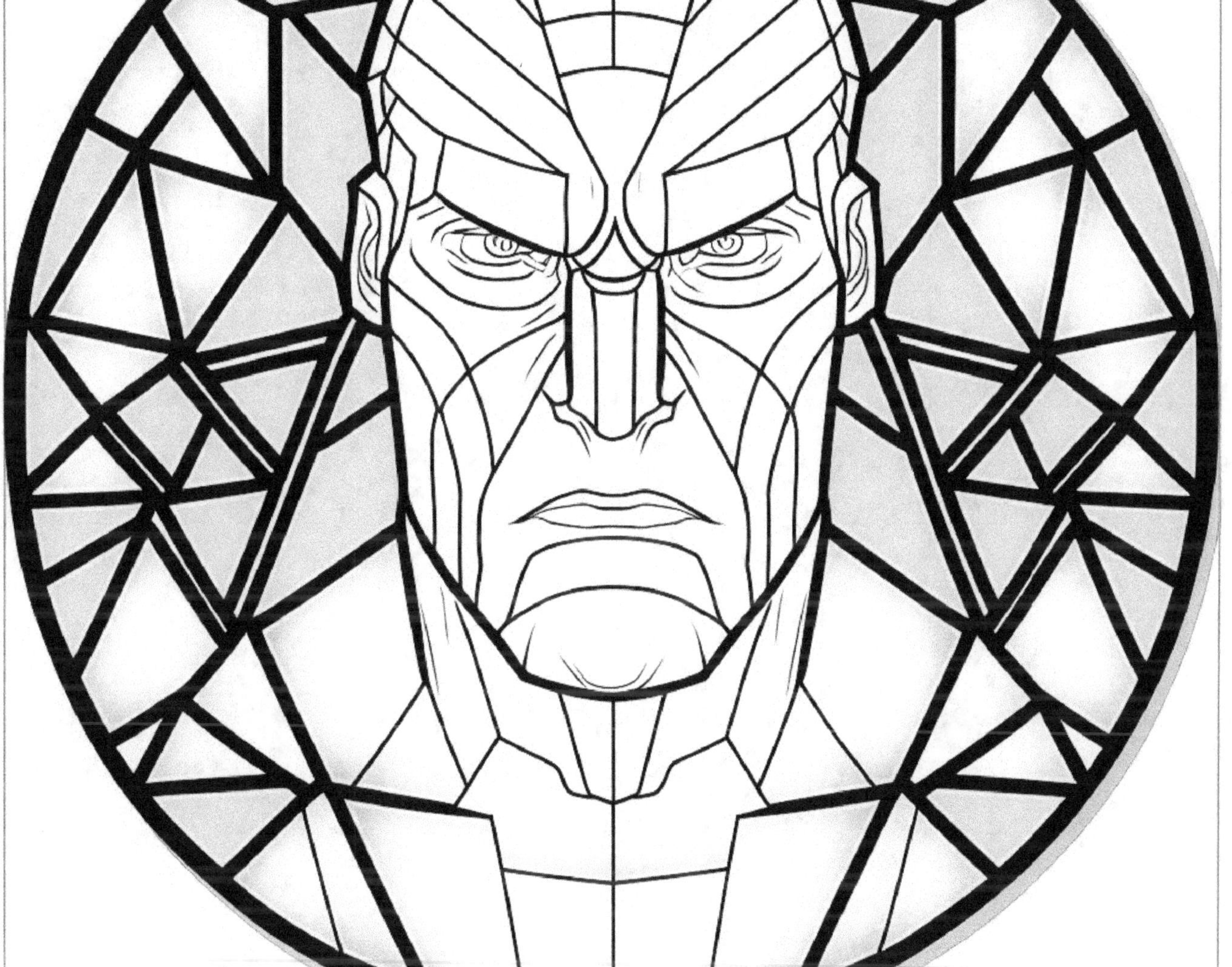
"TINEN MIAAN"

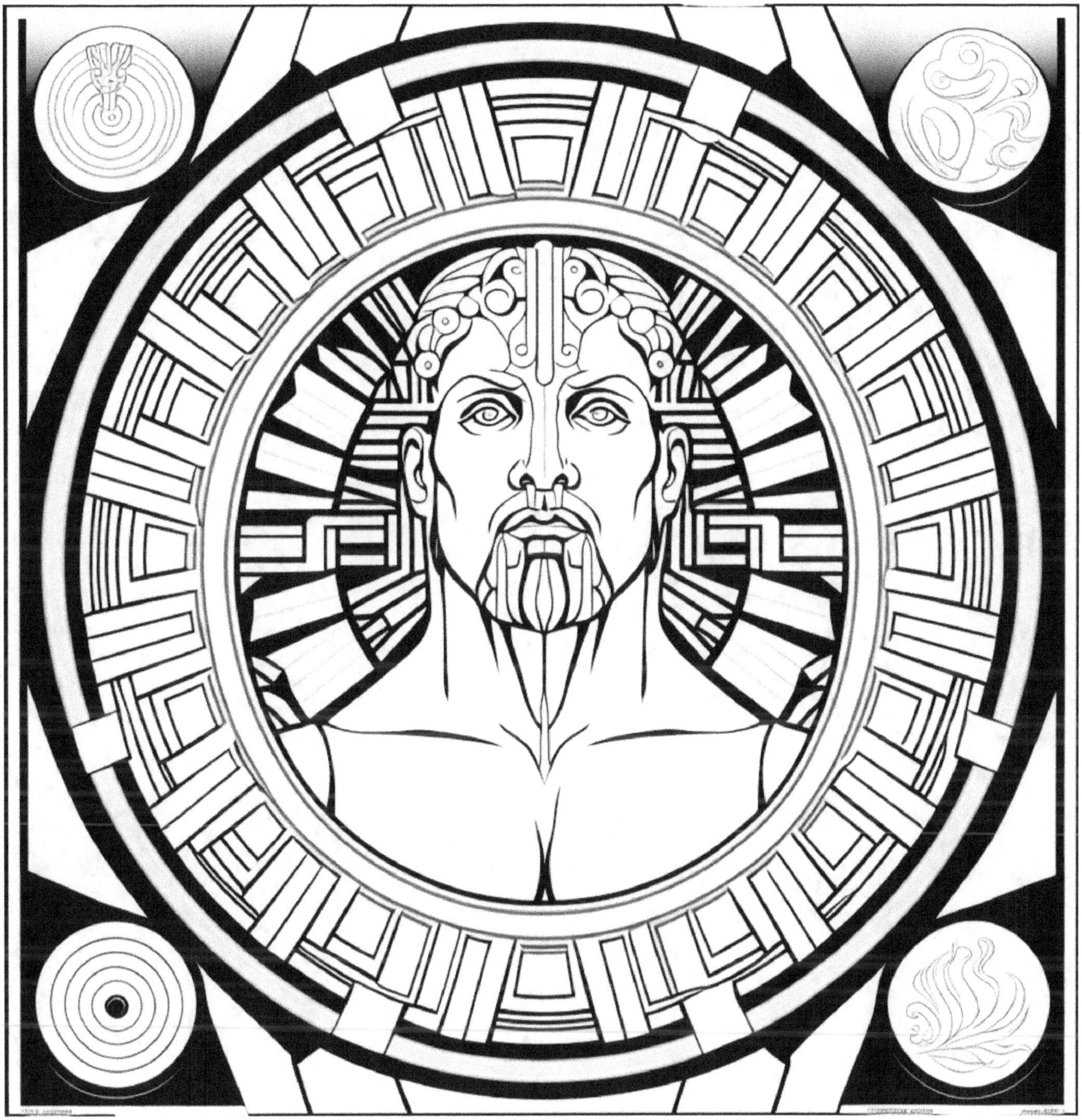

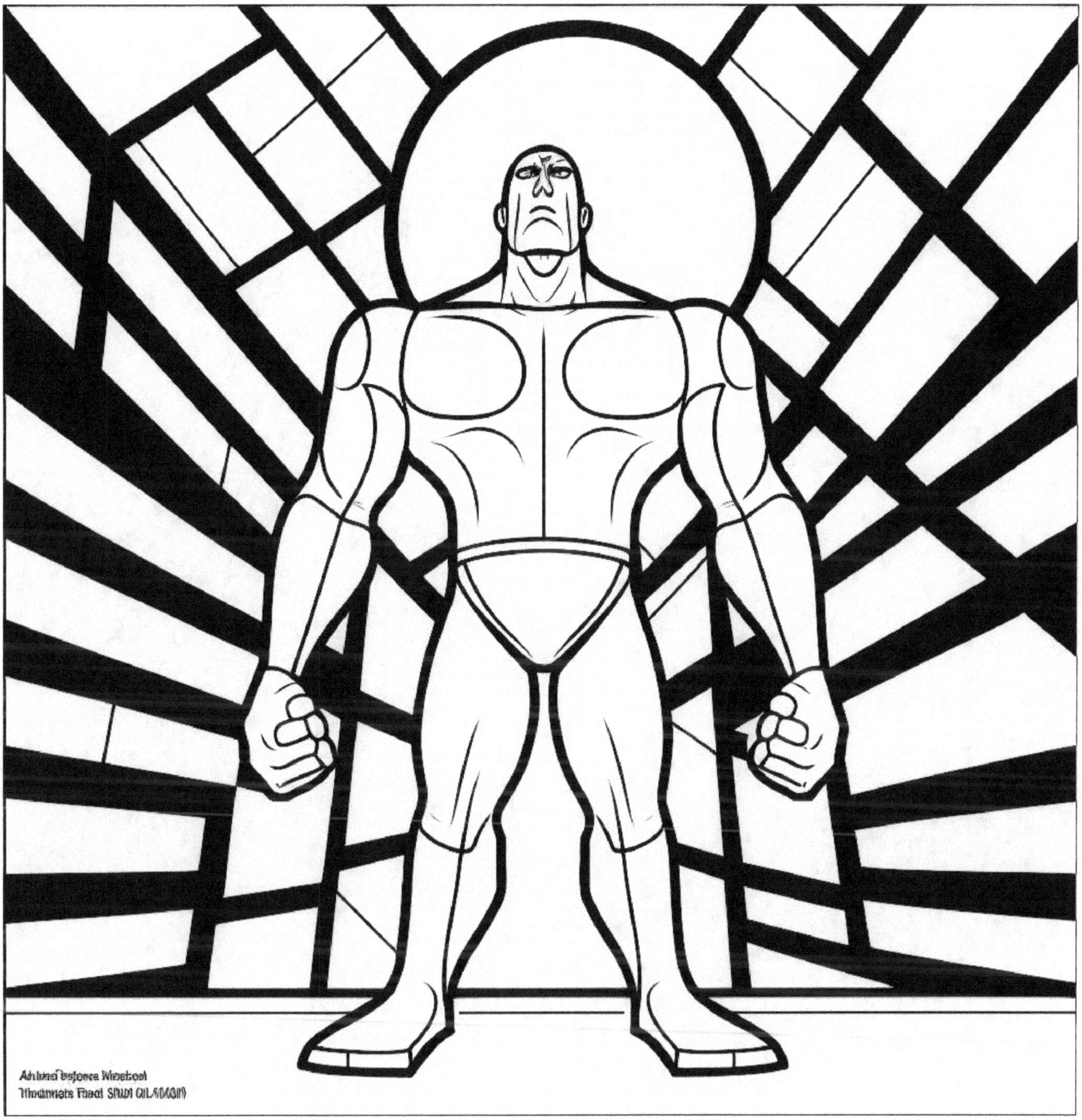

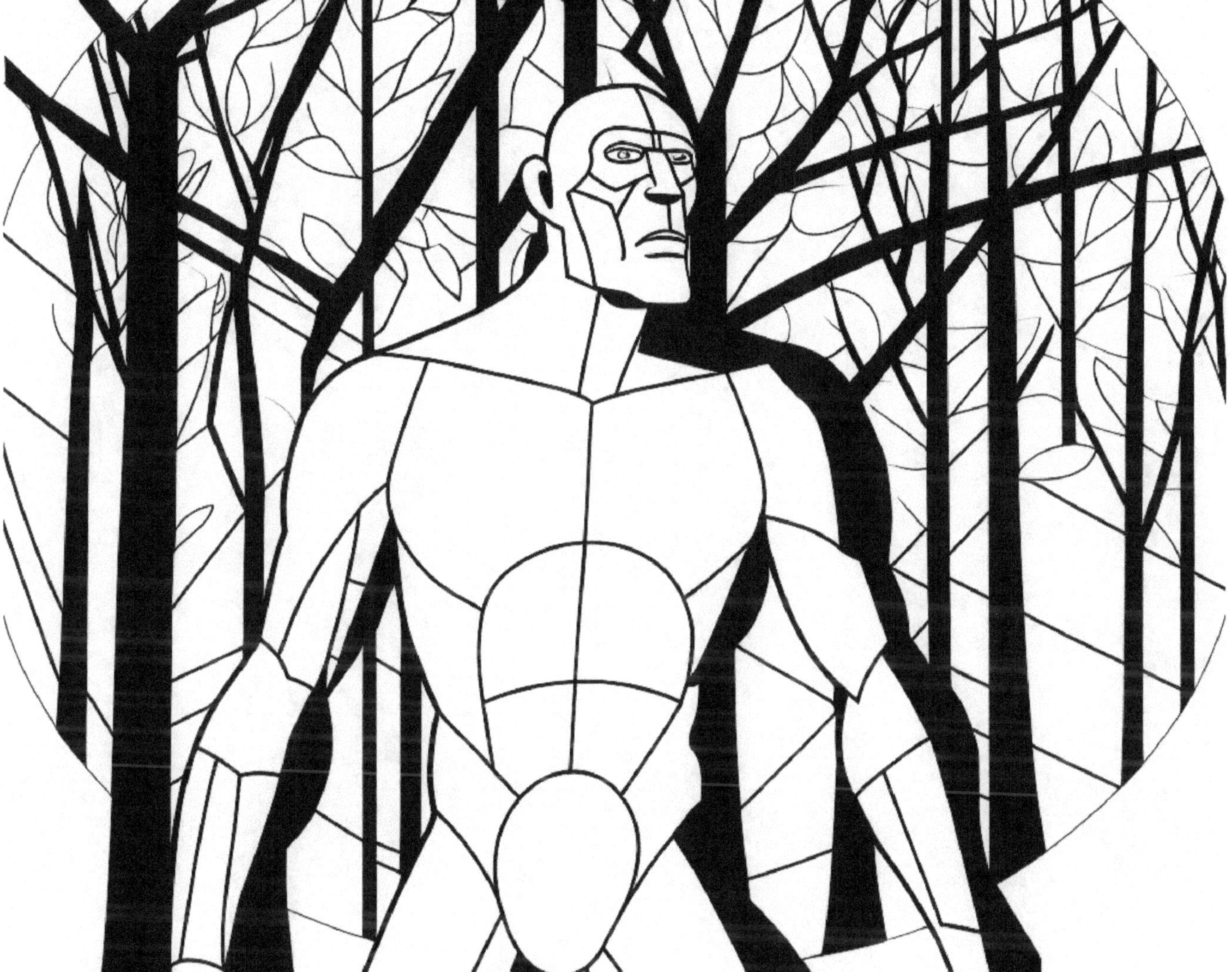

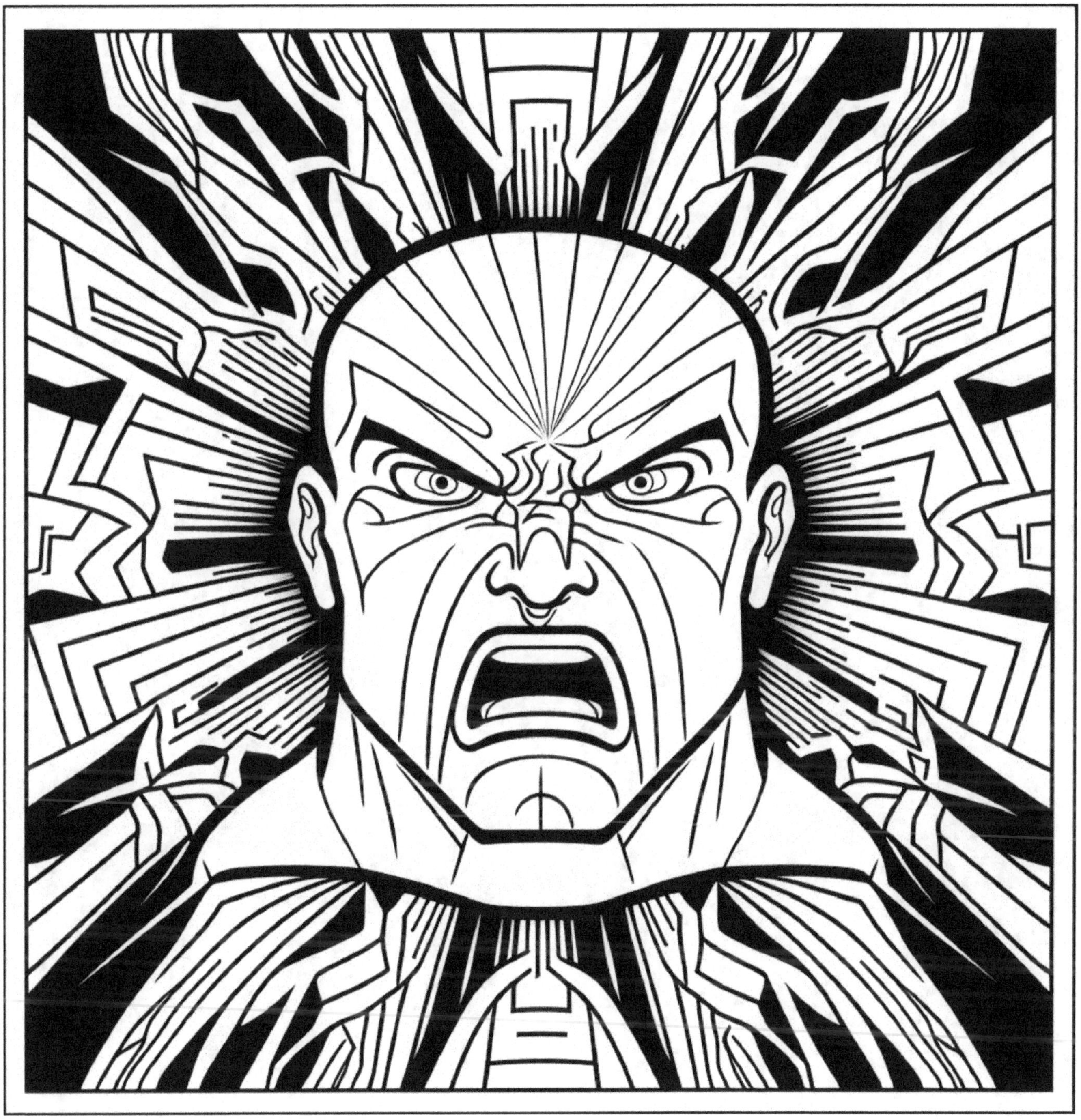

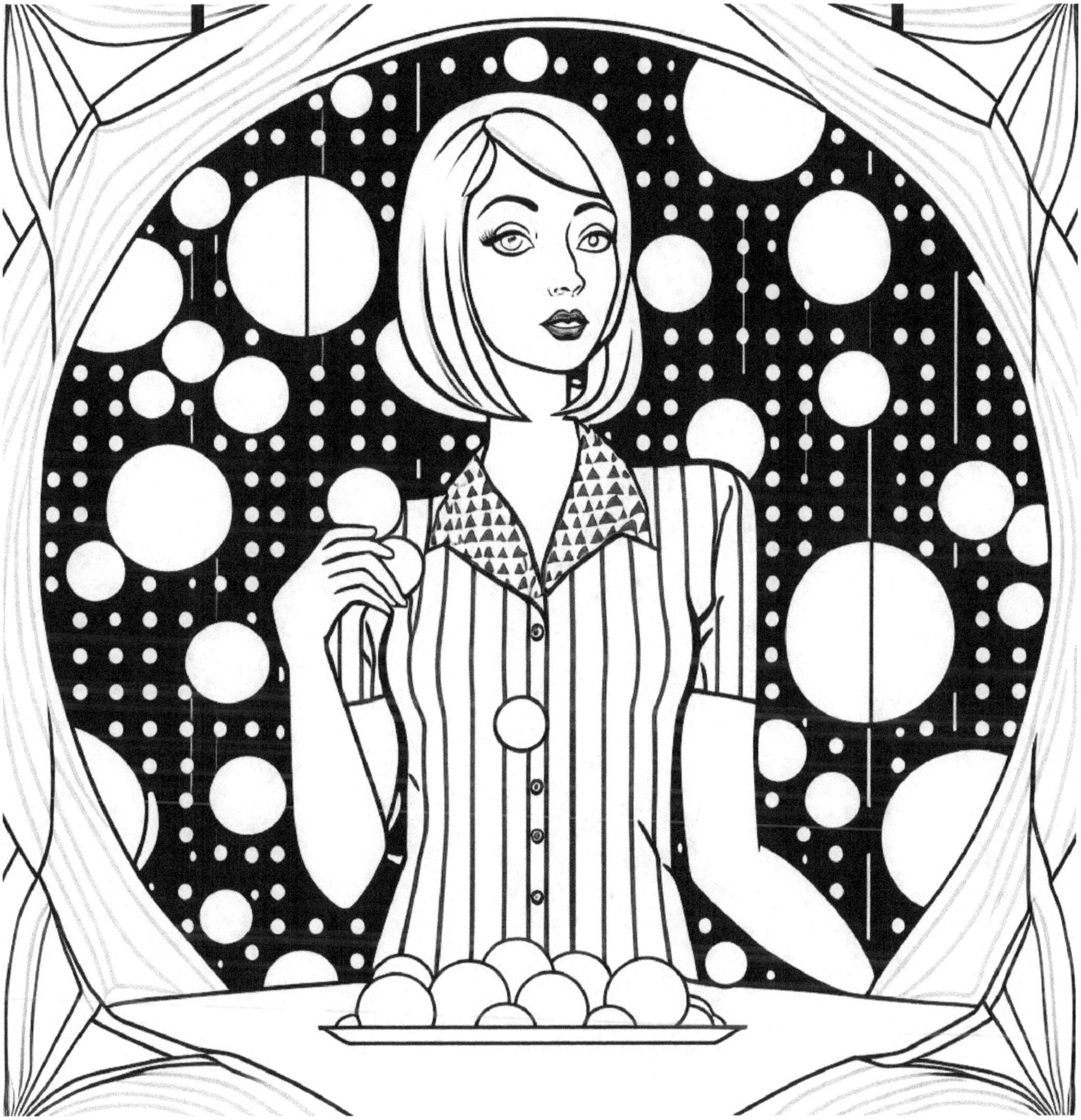

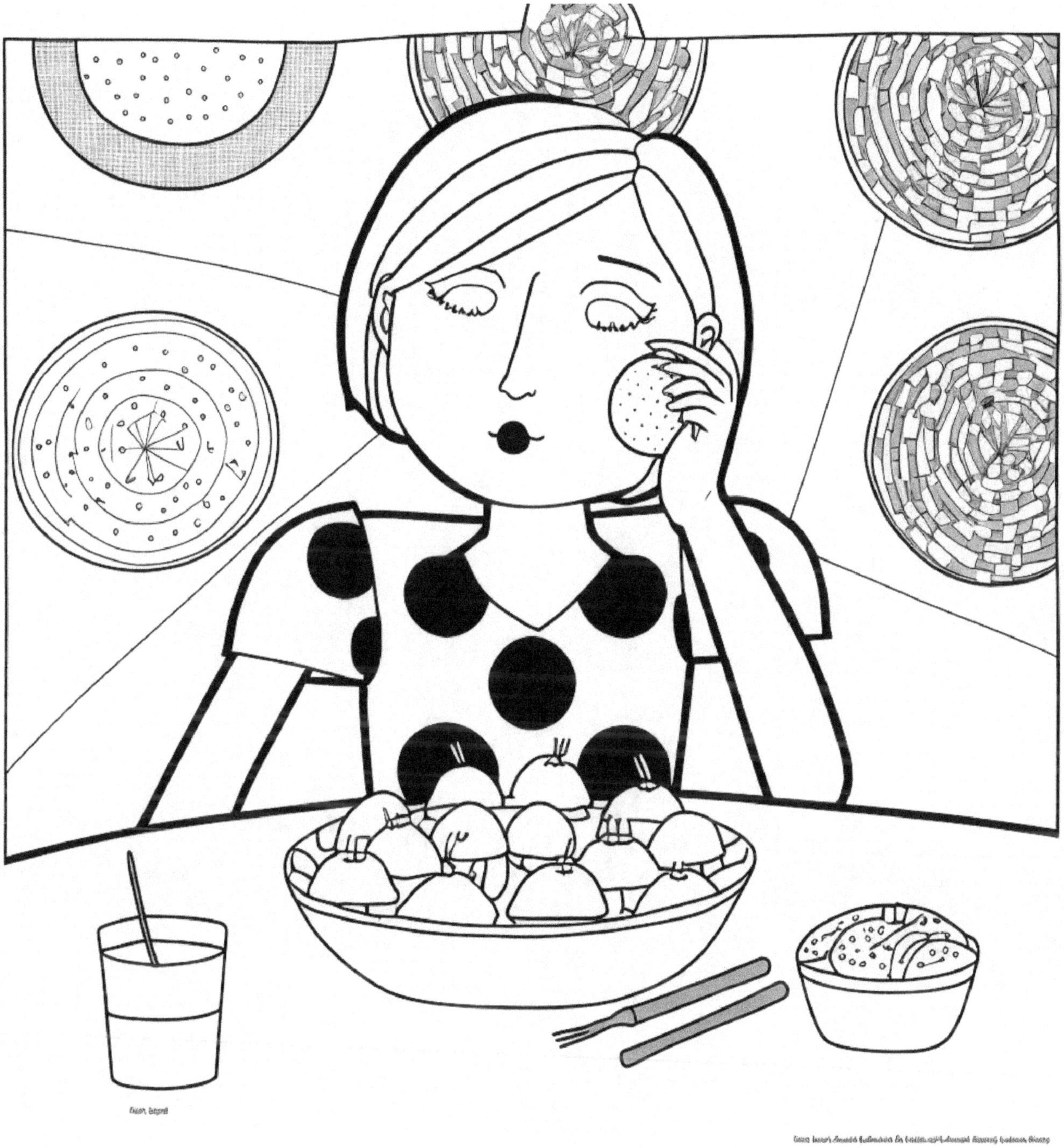

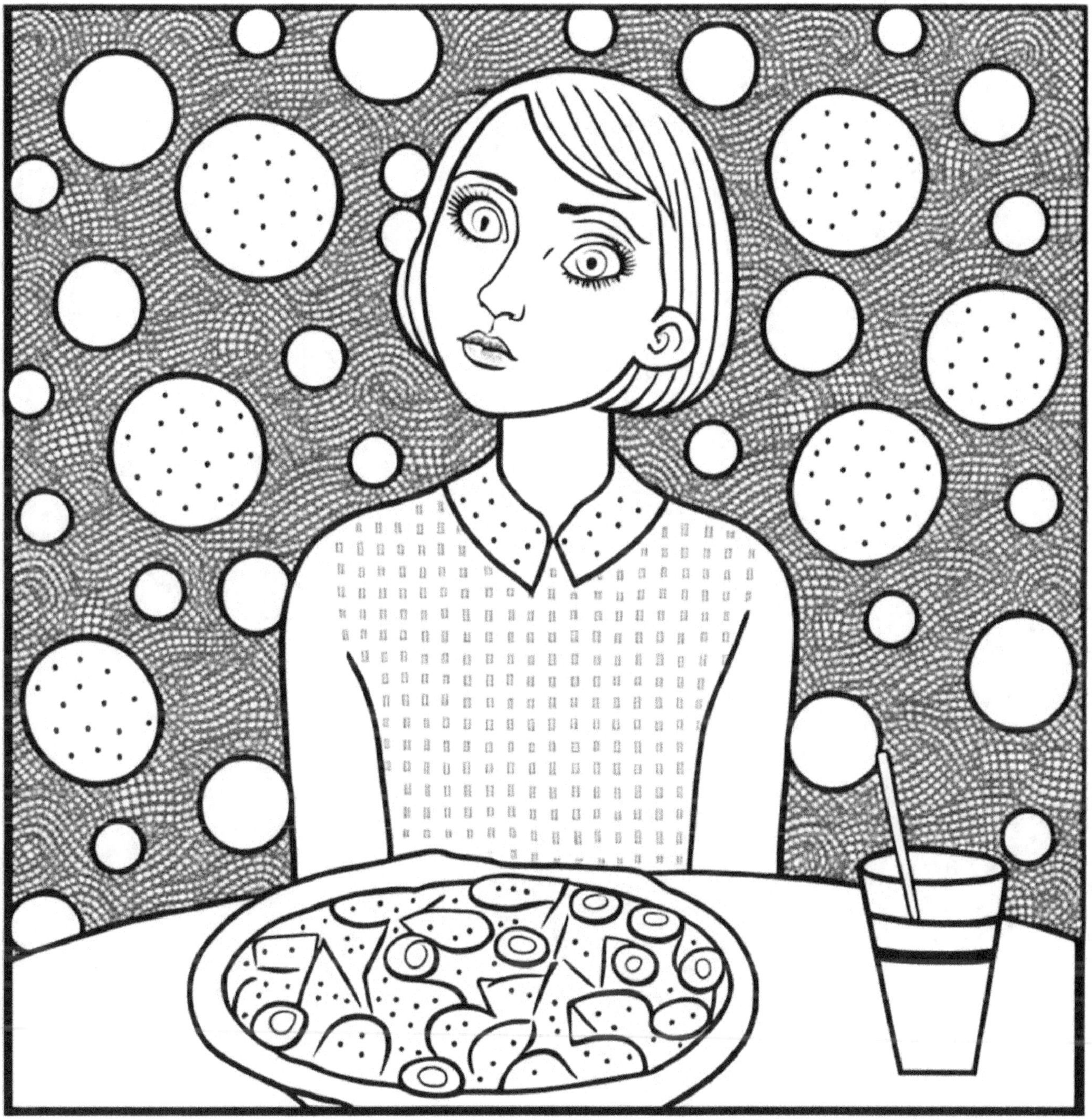

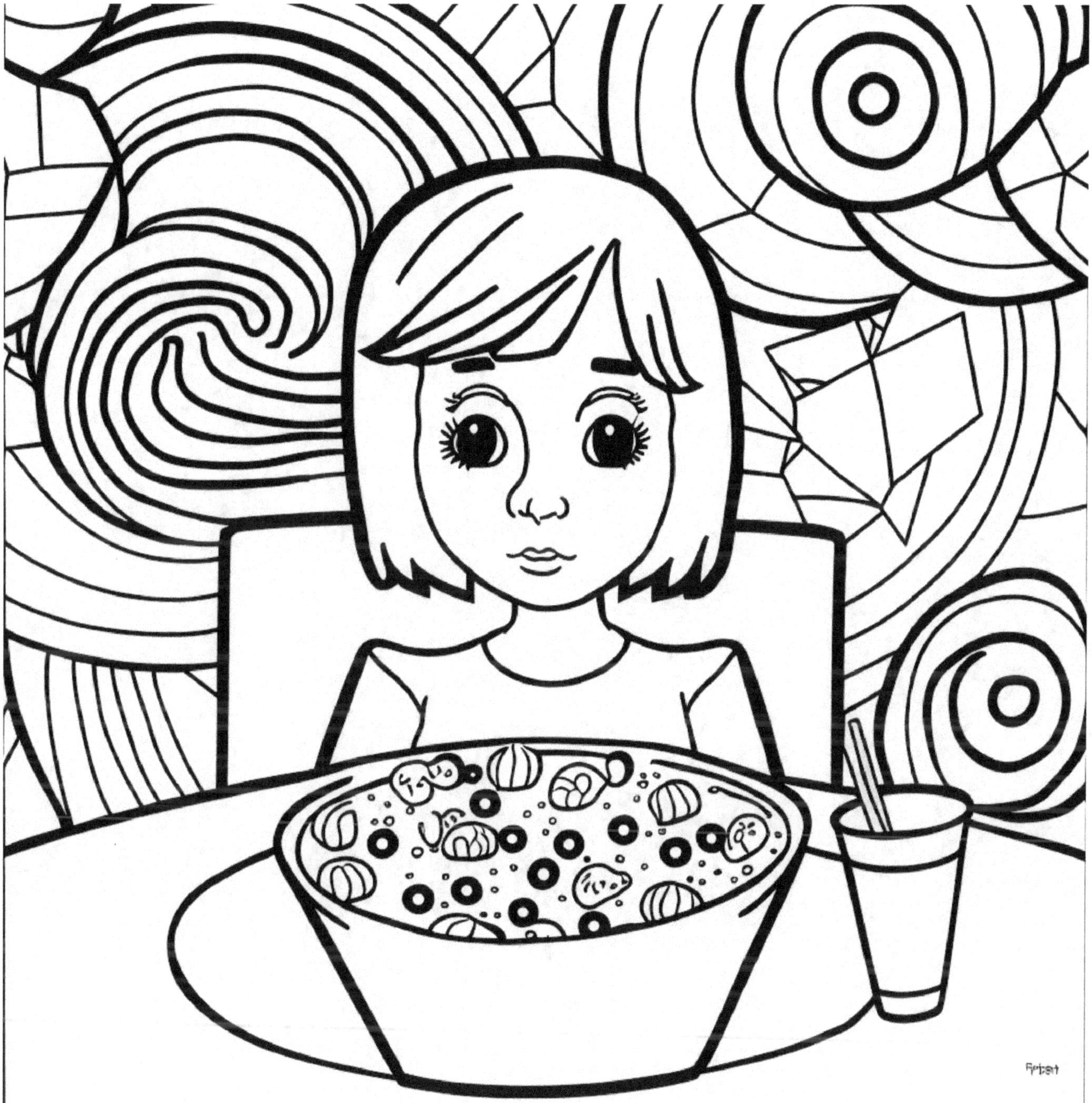

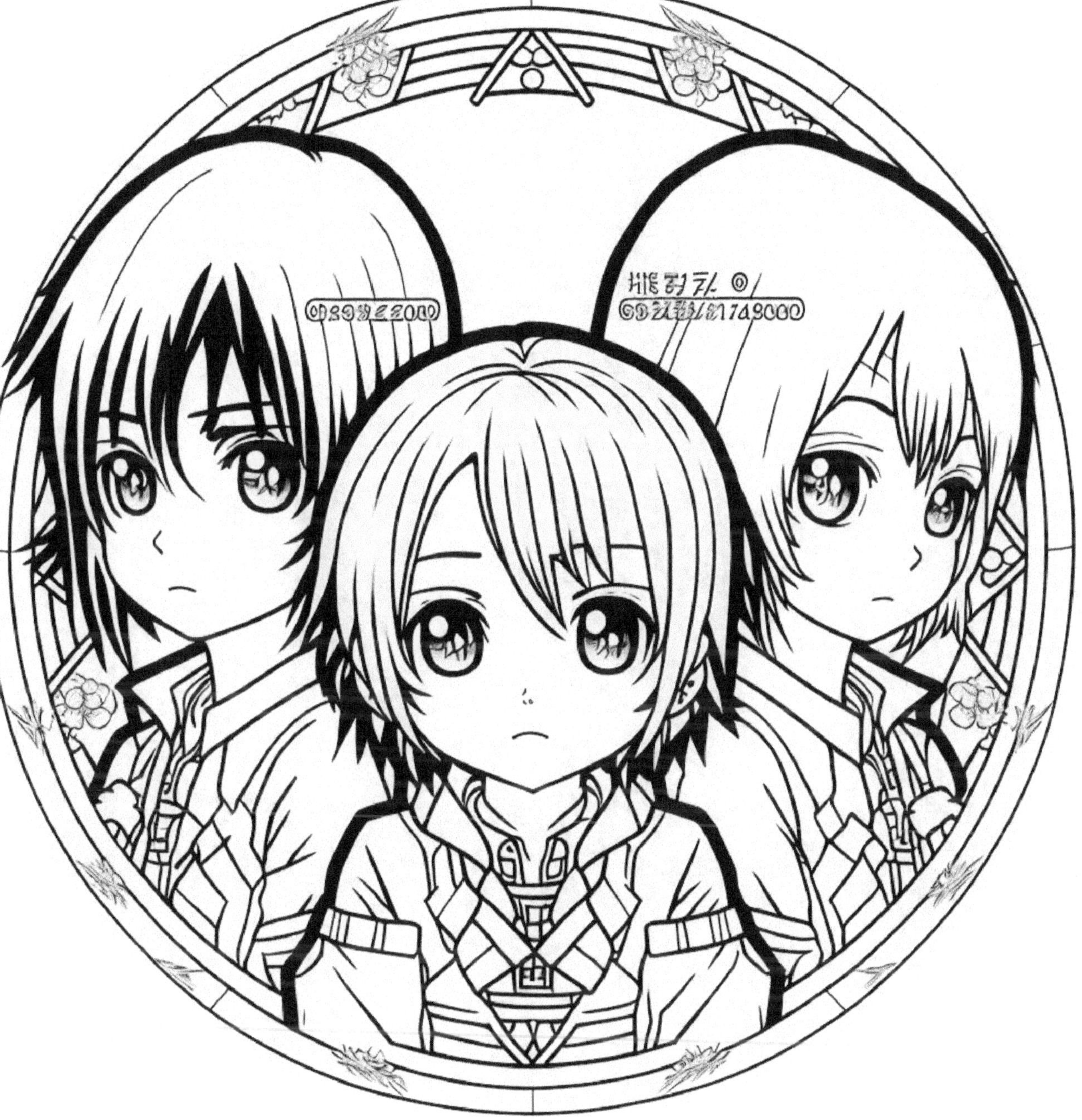

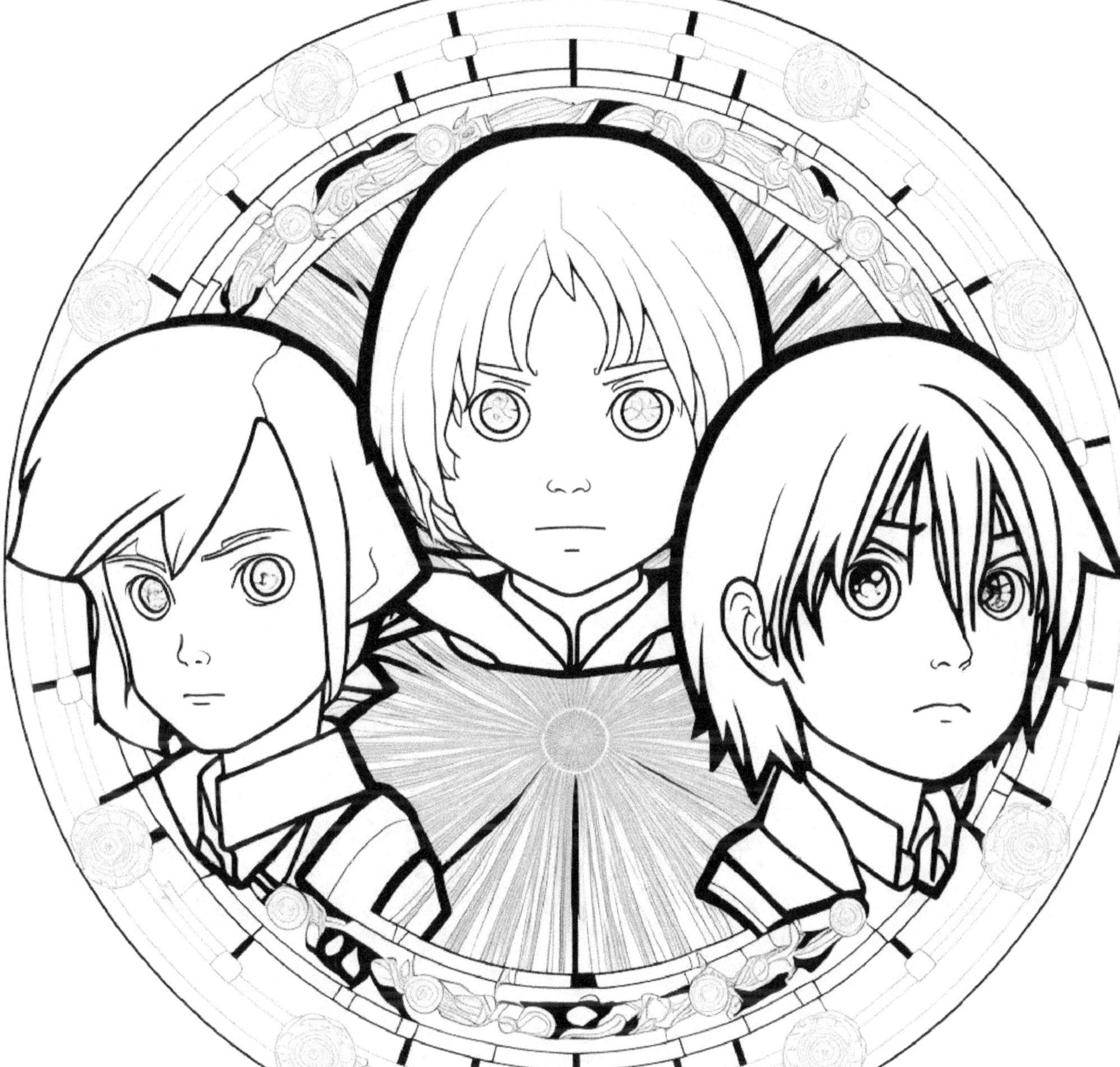

www.ingramcontent.com/pod-product-compliance
Lightning Source LLC
Chambersburg PA
CBHW080107010626
45794CB00015B/3298